LEARN GERMAN FOR BEGINNERS

OVER 300 CONVERSATIONAL DIALOGUES AND DAILY USED PHRASES TO LEARN GERMAN IN NO TIME. GROW YOUR VOCABULARY WITH GERMAN SHORT STORIES & LANGUAGE LEARNING LESSONS!

LANGUAGE MASTERY

Copyright © 2022 by Language Mastery

All rights reserved.

No part of this book may be reproduced in any form or by any electronic or mechanical means, including information storage and retrieval systems, without written permission from the author, except for the use of brief quotations in a book review.

CONTENTS

Introduction vii

1. THE WEEKEND TRIP 1
   Transition Words
   Summary 5
   Words to Remember 6
   Questions 7
   Answers 8
   English Translation 8

2. THE FORTUNE-TELLER 13
   Personal Pronouns, Possessive Pronouns & Possessive Adjectives
   Summary 18
   Words to Remember 18
   Questions 19
   Answers 20
   English Translation 21

3. THE HOTEL 27
   Common Everyday Objects
   Summary 32
   Words to Remember 32
   Questions 33
   Answers 34
   English Translation 35

4. SATURDAY 39
   Numbers
   Summary 42
   Words to Remember 42
   Questions 43

Answers	45
English Translation	45
5. BACK HOME *Relationship Words*	49
Summary	52
Words to Remember	52
Questions	53
Answers	55
English Translation	55
Conclusion	59
Also by Language Mastery	63

INTRODUCTION

Language is an irreplaceable part of human life. Just imagine for a moment that you wake up one morning and cannot speak your own language. How would your life be? How would you feel? Wouldn't life feel like a total mess? While knowing a language is essential, knowing more than one could be a competitive advantage for you. You will be able to communicate easily with more people and this can help you greatly in improving the quality of both your personal as well as professional life. What's more? Learning a new language is excellent for your brain. It is like a workout for the mind and can help you stay younger mentally.

Learning a new language isn't as hard as it seems. Learning can take place outside the classroom too. All you need is patience, lots of hard work, and regular practice. This book can be your guiding light and helping hand that you need on your language learning journey.

CREATED FOR BEGINNERS

This book is geared toward beginners. You will learn a new language through the adventures of Jack and Rose, a young British boy and a Swiss girl. It is divided into 17 chapters. As you walk with them through their various life experiences, you will not only be thoroughly entertained but will also get to learn loads of commonly used phrases and words to enrich your vocabulary.

This book can provide you with a really fun learning experience and will immerse you into a new language in the most interesting way.

THE BENEFITS OF LEARNING A NEW LANGUAGE

Learning a language is one of the most complete cognitive exercises: memory is activated while new neural connections are formed as we move from one language to another. Studying a foreign language increases language, reasoning, abstraction, and calculation skills. In addition to this, knowing more than one language opens up a whole new world to you: from being able to communicate with a larger audience, or opening your access to new job opportunities and relationships.

HOW TO USE THIS BOOK

Each chapter is divided into five sections. The first section contains the story. This is followed by a brief summary of the story. Next, you will find a list of important words that you must remember to increase your fluency, efficiency, and flow with this new language. Following this will be a section containing five questions based on the story. The final section will have answers to these questions. Whether you are 15 or 55, learning a new language using this book is going to be extremely easy and interesting.

Start by reading the story. Don't pressure yourself too much and just try to understand and absorb as much as you can in your first read. It is normal to not be able to understand every word. You are learning a new language after all. Read the summary next to confirm your understanding of the story. Try to remember the words/phrases listed under the "words to remember" category. Finally, check your knowledge and understanding by trying to answer the questions at the end of every chapter. Check your solutions with the answer key provided to see how many questions you got right. Try to learn from your mistakes and move on to the next chapter. As you progress from one chapter to the next, you will see your grasp of the new language gradually improve.

READ AND LISTEN

We highly recommend you buy the audio version of this book. If you choose to listen to the audiobook, you will hear a native German and English speaker narrating each story before or during reading. Reading along will help you become accustomed to their accent, which will be helpful when applying your new language skills in real-life situations.

Don't wait anymore. Put all your fears and apprehension away and set foot on this amazing language learning journey today!

1

THE WEEKEND TRIP

TRANSITION WORDS

Jack und Rose sind im Auto. Jacks Handy klingelt und er nimmt ab.

"Hallo!"

Der Mann auf der anderen Seite sagt etwas, worauf er antwortet: „Ich denke in etwa fünfzehn Minuten."

„Sie müssen ihn fragen, wie weit wir von unserem Ziel entfernt sind! **Aber** wer fragt ihn das?" wundert sich Rose.

„Wir haben zwei Taschen. Wir sind zu zweit, also jeder eine Tasche", sagt Jack zu dem Mann.

"Zwei Taschen! Heißt das, wir nehmen ein Flugzeug? Ich habe ihm gesagt, er soll keine Flugzeuge oder Züge buchen!", denkt sich Rose.

"Sicher! Vielen Dank."

Jack legt auf.

Er sieht Rose an und sie lächelt. Er sagt nichts und beide verbringen ihre Zeit damit, die vorbeiziehende Landschaft zu beobachten.

„Autofahrten sind eine hervorragende Möglichkeit, die wahre Schönheit der Natur eines Landes zu sehen! Italien ist sehr schön", sagt Jack.

"**In der Tat**! Hier gibt es **so** viele schöne Fotomotive", bemerkt Rose.

„Wo wir hingehen, wird es noch so viele mehr geben", sagt Jack.

"Wirklich? Ich freue mich riesig auf die Überraschung!
"

„Ich hoffe, du wirst angenehm überrascht sein!", sagt Jack und drückt die Daumen.

"Mach dir keine Sorgen! Es wird alles gut!", sagt Rose. „Es wird jetzt keine Pannen mehr geben", fügt sie hinzu.

„Das hoffe ich", sagt Jack.

Plötzlich kommt das Auto mitten auf der Straße zum Stehen.

"Was ist passiert?", fragt Jack den Fahrer.

„Ich glaube, es gibt ein Problem mit dem Motor", antwortet der Fahrer.

"Oh Gott! Nicht noch einmal!", sagt Rose irritiert. „Was machen wir jetzt auf dieser verlassenen Straße? Wie werden wir unser Ziel erreichen?", fügt sie hinzu.

„Wir sind mitten auf der Straße! Wir müssen das Auto zu**erst** zur Seite schieben", sagt Jack leise.

"Ja, ja! Können Sie mir bitte helfen?", fragt der Fahrer Jack.

"Sicher!", sagt Jack. Rose steigt aus dem Auto und die beiden Männer schieben das Fahrzeug an den Straßenrand.

"Lassen Sie mich jetzt das Auto inspizieren!", sagt der Fahrer und öffnet die Motorhaube.

Rose ist sehr aufgebracht. „Du hast gesagt, du magst Abenteuer, oder?", sagt Jack mit einem Lächeln.

„Ja, aber nicht schon wieder so etwas. Das ist das **zweite** Mal, dass wir auf halbem Weg festsitzen."

"Mach dir keine Sorgen! Wir werden unser Ziel **trotz** aller Hürden erreichen. Genieße jedes Stück der Reise.

Schließlich sind es Momente wie diese, die eine Reise unvergesslich machen", versichert Jack ihr.

„Es gibt ein Problem mit der Batterie. Ich muss einen Mechaniker rufen", unterbricht der Fahrer.

"Wie lange wird das dauern?", fragt Jack.

„**Da** wir uns an einem abgelegenen Ort befinden, kann es einige Zeit dauern, einen Mechaniker zu bekommen. **Allerdings** bezweifle ich, dass der Mechaniker das Problem hier beheben kann", sagt der Fahrer.

„Wollen Sie damit sagen, dass die Reparatur länger als eine Stunde dauern wird?", fragt Jack.

"**Ohne Zweifel**. Vielleicht möchte der Mechaniker das Auto sogar in seine Werkstatt bringen, um die Reparatur dort durchzuführen."

"Oh nein! Was machen wir **dann**?", sagt Rose enttäuscht.

„Ähm… Sie können versuchen, ein anderes Taxi zu buchen. **Falls** es Ihnen nichts ausmacht, etwas zu warten, können Sie hier bleiben, bis der Mechaniker kommt, und sehen, was er sagt. **Denn so oder so** müssen Sie warten, auch wenn Sie ein anderes Taxi buchen", schlägt der Fahrer vor.

„Ich denke, es ist keine schlechte Idee, zu warten", sagt Jack und sieht Rose an.

„Okay, aber was machen wir hier so lange? Es wird auch dunkel", sagt Rose.

„**Wenn** Sie nicht auf Ihr Reiseziels festgelegt sind, habe ich eine Idee! Es gibt ein Hotel in der Nähe. Sie können dort über Nacht bleiben und dann morgen früh zu Ihrem Zielort aufbrechen", sagt der Fahrer.

"Keine schlechte Idee, Rose!", sagt Jack.

„Das Leben ist wirklich unberechenbar! Wir haben uns **aus diesem Grund** entschieden, Zug und Flugzeug zu meiden, und diese Hürden verfolgen uns auch hier. Das ist so ungerecht", sagt Rose.

„**Selbst wenn** dies nicht der Ort ist, an dem wir sein wollten, können wir hier **letztendlich** die gleichen Abenteuer erleben", sagt Jack.

"Wie?", fragt Rose.

„Was ich geplant hatte, war ein Campingausflug im Wald. Und ich habe gerade mit Hilfe von Herrn Google entdeckt, dass es hier auch einen Wald gibt. Obwohl es natürlich nicht dasselbe sein wird, können wir letztlich den gleichen Spaß haben", sagt Jack.

Rose stimmt sofort zu. Sie ist wieder glücklich.

„Ich habe gerade eine Nachricht von meiner Firma erhalten. Der Mechaniker wird in etwa 30 Minuten da sein", sagt der Fahrer.

"Das ist wunderbar!", sagt Rose.

„Der Mechaniker hat ein Auto, also werde ich Sie mit seinem Auto zum Hotel bringen. Er ist ein sehr netter Mann. Das macht ihm nichts aus", sagt der Fahrer.

"Vielen Dank."

Jack lächelt.

„Hier gibt es einige interessante Dinge zu tun, wenn Sie interessiert sind", sagt der Fahrer.

"Was **zum Beispiel**?", fragt Rose.

„Es sind Kleinigkeiten, nichts Großes. Etwa einen Kilometer nördlich von hier gibt es zum Beispiel einen schönen Picknickplatz. Da ist dieser Wald, von dem Sie gerade gesprochen haben. Hier gibt es auch einige Bauernhöfe, wenn Sie das Dorfleben erleben möchten. Und **zuletzt** gibt es in der Nähe einen netten Wahrsager, der wirklich erstaunlich gut darin ist, die Zukunft vorherzusagen. Diese Aktivitäten könnten ein netter Zeitvertreib für Sie beide sein, **während** Sie auf die Ankunft des Mechanikers warten. Hier gibt es auch einen kleinen Wasserpark. Aber

aufgrund der Zerstörungen durch den Sturm ist er nicht mehr in Betrieb", sagt der Fahrer.

"Wahrsager! Wow! Das klingt wirklich interessant!", sagt Rose.

„Was sagst du, Jack? Sollen wir jetzt dorthin gehen?"

„Ähm... In Ordnung! Ich glaube nicht an Wahrsagerei, aber es kann sicher unterhaltsam sein", sagt Jack.

"Definitiv! Sie werden Ihre Zeit mit ihm genießen! Er wohnt in der Nähe", bemerkt der Fahrer.

„**Endlich** etwas Spannendes zu tun!", sagt Rose.

Jack lächelt und sagt zum Fahrer: „Können Sie uns bitte den Weg zu seiner Wohnung zeigen?"

„Sie sind neu hier und die Strecke ist etwas kompliziert. Deshalb ist es besser, wenn Sie mir folgen. Ich bringe Sie hin. Es ist nicht sehr weit", antwortet der Fahrer.

Jack und Rose stimmen zu und der Fahrer führt sie zum Haus des Wahrsagers.

SUMMARY

Jack und Rose sind im Auto. Sie sind auf dem Weg zu einem Ziel, welches eine Überraschung für Rose sein soll. Das Auto hält plötzlich auf halber Strecke an und der Fahrer sagt, dass es lange dauern wird, das Problem zu beheben. Der Fahrer gibt ihnen mehrere alternative Lösungen. Jack und Rose beschließen schließlich, die Nacht in einem nahe gelegenen Hotel zu verbringen und am Wochenende den Wald zu erkunden.

WORDS TO REMEMBER

1. **Aber** - But
2. **So** - So
3. **Plötzlich** - All of a sudden
4. **Zuerst** - First
5. **Zweite** - Second
6. **Trotz** - Despite
7. **Da** - Since
8. **Jedoch** - However
9. **Ohne Zweifel** - Without a doubt
10. **Letztendlich** - Eventually
11. **Während** - While
12. **In der Tat** - In fact
13. **Dann** - Then
14. **Wenn** - If
15. **Denn** - Because
16. **So oder so** - Either way
17. **Schließlich** - After all
18. **Aus diesem Grund** - For this reason
19. **Selbst wenn** - Even though
20. **Letztendlich** - Ultimately
21. **Zum Beispiel** - For example
22. **Zuletzt** - Lastly
23. **Aufgrund** - Due to
24. **Endlich** - Finally
25. **Deshalb** - Therefore

QUESTIONS

1. Wie viele Taschen haben Jack und Rose insgesamt?

- a. Zwei
- b. Vier
- c. Sechs
- d. Acht

2. Was passiert auf halber Strecke?

- a. Jack und Rose beginnen zu streiten
- b. Der Fahrer wird krank
- c. Das Auto hält plötzlich an
- d. Jack und Rose halten zum Abendessen in einem Restaurant an

3. Wie reagiert Rose, als das Auto plötzlich anhält?

- a. Sie ist sehr glücklich
- b. Sie weint
- c. Sie schreit den Fahrer an
- d. Sie ist aufgebracht

4. Welcher der folgenden Orte ist wegen der Zerstörung durch den Sturm geschlossen?

- a. Der Flughafen
- b. Der Wasserpark
- c. Das Hotel
- d. Der Bahnhof

5. Welche der folgenden Möglichkeiten findet Rose interessant?

- a. Einen Besuch bei dem Wahrsager
- b. Einen Urlaub in Amerika
- c. Einen Tag im Wasserpark
- d. Japanisches Essen in einem Restaurant essen

ANSWERS

1. **a.** Zwei
2. **c.** Das Auto hält plötzlich an
3. **d.** Sie ist aufgebracht
4. **b.** Der Wasserpark
5. **a.** Einen Besuch bei dem Wahrsager

ENGLISH TRANSLATION

Jack and Rose are in the car. Jack's mobile phone rings and he answers.

"Hello!"

The man on the other side says something to which he replies, "I think in about fifteen minutes."

"They must be asking him how far we are from the destination! But who is asking him that?" Rose wonders.

"We have two bags. There are two of us, so one bag each." Jack says to the man.

"Two bags! Does this mean we are taking a plane! I told him not to book any planes or trains!" Rose thinks to herself.

"Sure! Thank you."

Jack hangs up.

He looks at Rose and she smiles. He says nothing and both of them spend their time observing the passing scenery.

"Car journeys are an excellent way to see the real natural beauty of a country! Italy is very beautiful." Jack says.

"Indeed! There are so many lovely photo opportunities here," Rose remarks.

"There are going to be so many more where we're going," says Jack.

"Really? I am so excited about the surprise!"

"I hope you are pleasantly surprised!" Jack says and crosses his fingers.

"Don't worry! It will all be good!" Rose says. "There are not going to be any more mishaps now," she adds.

"I hope so," Jack says.

All of a sudden, the car comes to a stop in the middle of the road.

"What happened?" Jack asks the driver.

"I think there is a problem with the engine," the driver replies.

"Oh, God! Not again!" Rose says, irritated. "What will

we do now on this deserted road? How will we reach our destination?" she adds.

"We are in the middle of the road! We first need to push the car to the side," Jack says quietly.

"Yes, yes! Could you please help me, sir?" the driver asks Jack.

"Sure!" says Jack. Rose steps out of the car, and the two men push the vehicle to the side of the road.

"Let me inspect the car!" the driver says and opens the bonnet.

Rose is very upset. "You said you like adventures, right?" Jack says with a smile.

"Yes, but not this again. This is the second time we are getting stuck halfway."

"Don't worry! We will reach our destination despite all the hurdles. Enjoy every bit of the journey. After all, it's moments like these that make a trip memorable," Jack assures her.

"There is a problem with the battery. I will have to call a mechanic," interrupts the driver.

"How long will this take?" Jack asks.

"Since we are in a remote location, it might take some time to get a mechanic. However, I doubt the mechanic will be able to correct the problem here," says the driver.

"Are you saying this will take more than an hour to rectify?" Jack asks.

"Without a doubt. In fact, the mechanic may even want to take the car to his shop to do the repair."

"Oh no! What will we do then?" Rose says disappointed.

"Uhm. You may try booking another cab. If you don't mind waiting a bit, you can stay here until the mechanic arrives and see what he says. Because either way, you will have to wait even if you choose to book another cab," suggests the driver.

"I think it's not a bad idea to wait," Jack says and looks at Rose.

"Ok, but what will we do here for so long? It's also getting dark." Rose says.

"If you are not particular about your destination, I have an idea! There is a hotel nearby. You can stay there for the night and then leave for your destination tomorrow morning. " says the driver.

"It's not a bad idea, Rose!" Jack says.

"Life is truly unpredictable! We decided to avoid trains and planes for this reason, and these hurdles are following us here as well. This is so unfair." Rose says.

"Even though this place isn't where we wanted to be, we can ultimately experience the same adventures here," Jack says.

"How?" Rose asks.

"What I had planned was a camping trip in the forest. And I just discovered with the help of Mr. Google that there is a forest here too. While it will obviously not be the same as that one, it can eventually give us the same kind of fun experience." Jack says.

Rose immediately agrees. She is happy again.

"I just received a message from my company. The mechanic will be here in about 30 minutes," says the driver.

"That's wonderful!" Rose says.

"The mechanic will have a car, so I will drop you off at the hotel in his car. He's a very nice man. He won't mind," says the driver.

"Thank you very much."

Jack smiles.

"There are some interesting things to do here if you're interested," the driver says.

"Like what?" asks Rose.

"They are small things, not anything major. For example, about a mile north of here, there is a beautiful picnic spot. There is that forest you just spoke about. There are some farms here too if you want to experience village life. And lastly, there is a nice fortune-teller nearby who is really amazing at predicting the future. These activities could be a nice pastime for you both while you wait for the mechanic to arrive. There is also a small water park here. But as a result of the destruction caused by the storm, it is no longer operational," says the driver.

"fortune-teller! Wow! That sounds really interesting!" Rose says. "What do you say, Jack? Shall we go there now?"

"Uhm. All right! I don't believe in fortune-telling, but it can be entertaining," Jack says.

"Definitely! You will enjoy your time with him! He lives close by," remarks the driver.

"Finally, something exciting to do!" Rose says.

Jack smiles and tells the driver, "Can you please show us the way to his place?"

"You are new here, and the route is a bit complicated. Therefore, it is better that you follow me. I will take you there. It is not very far." the driver replies.

Jack and Rose agree, and the driver leads the way to the fortune-teller's house.

2

THE FORTUNE-TELLER

PERSONAL PRONOUNS, POSSESSIVE PRONOUNS & POSSESSIVE ADJECTIVES

Das Wetter ist angenehm, die Sonne geht unter und die Straße ist ruhig. Jack, Rose und der Fahrer gehen auf das Haus des Wahrsagers zu. Der Klang **ihrer** Schritte hallt wider. Der Fahrer geht zügig **vor ihnen** her. **Er** scheint sehr fit zu sein. Jack kann mit seiner Geschwindigkeit mithalten, Rose jedoch nicht. Einer **ihrer** Schuhe ist kaputt.

„Wie willst **du** in diesen Schuhen laufen? **Dein** anderer Schuh wird auch sehr bald kaputtgehen", sagt Jack lachend.

„Pst! Sag das nicht, Jack! Wenn **mein** anderer Schuh auch kaputtgeht, bekomme **ich** ernsthafte Probleme", sagt Rose.

"Welche Schuhgröße hast du?", sagt Jack und schaut auf ihre winzigen Füße.

"Meine Schuhgröße? Ich weiß, sie ist ziemlich klein", sagt Rose lächelnd.

„Am Rande des Dorfes, in dem **wir** waren, gab es einen sehr schönen Laden. **Sie** hatten auch eine gute Schuhkollektion, aber in diesem Laden gab es keine Kinderabteilung!", bemerkt Jack lachend.

"**Du** machst dich über **mich** lustig! Ich bin das größte Mädchen in **unserer** Familie", sagt Rose lächelnd.

"Wow! Herzlichen Glückwünsch!", sagt Jack.

Sie lacht.

„Wir werden jetzt diese Gasse auf der linken Seite hinuntergehen. **Es** ist ein bisschen steinig, aber es ist der kürzeste Weg", sagt der Fahrer.

„Alles Gute für dich und **deine** Lieben für den weiteren Weg!", sagt Jack und lächelt Rose an.

„Meine Schuhe machen bis jetzt einen tollen Job! Ich schaffe das", sagt Rose, aber er zweifelt.

„Dein anderer Schuh scheint in keinem guten Zustand zu sein. Ich glaube, seine Sohle löst sich auf einer Seite ab", sagt er.

"Nein, alles in Ordnung. Ich schaffe es bis zum Haus des Wahrsagers", sagt sie.

Die Straße ist jetzt sehr schmal und die drei gehen weiter. Es gibt ein paar weit auseinanderliegende Häuser, und der Fahrer zeigt auf das letzte. Das Haus ist nicht allzu groß, aber **es ist** das größte in dieser Gasse. Die Tür ist leicht geöffnet, und durch den Türspalt kann man eine Kristallkugel sehen. Der Fahrer klopft an die Tür und ruft:

"Herr Burgundy! Ich bin es, Paul."

„Oh, hallo Paul! Bitte kommen Sie herein." antwortet der Wahrsager.

„Sie haben zwei Besucher. Ich habe sie mitgebracht."

Jack und Rose hören das Geräusch eines Stuhls, der über den Boden gezogen wird, und dann Schritte. Herr Burgundy kommt zur Tür. Er begrüßt Jack und Rose und sie folgen ihm hinein. Jack gefällt der Ort nicht. Er fühlt sich nicht wohl, aber er sagt nichts. Der Wahrsager führt sie in einen Raum, in dem ein Tisch und Stühle stehen.

„Bitte nehmen Sie Platz", sagt der Wahrsager.

„Genießen Sie diese Sitzung. Ich werde im Auto

warten. Der Mechaniker wird gleich da sein", sagt der Fahrer und geht.

Jack und Rose setzen sich und der Wahrsager sitzt ihnen gegenüber.

„Okay, wer möchte anfangen?", fragt der Mann.

"Ich!", antwortet Rose antwortet.

Der Wahrsager lacht und bittet sie, ihm ihre Hand zu reichen.

„Sie sind also ein Handleser. Benutzten Sie keine Kristallkugel?", fragt Jack.

Rose ist verwirrt. Sie hat keine Ahnung vom Handlesen oder von Kristallkugeln.

"Ja! Ich benutze beides", sagt der Wahrsager.

Rose streckt ihre Handfläche aus und sagt: „Ich bin bereit."

Der Wahrsager untersucht sorgfältig ihre Handfläche und die verschiedenen Linien darauf. Er zeichnet etwas auf ein Blatt Papier.

„Sie sind ein Mädchen, das viel Glück hat! Sie sind sehr künstlerisch. Arbeiten Sie in der Kunstbranche?", fragt er.

Rose ist sehr beeindruckt. "Ja, tatsächlich!" sagt sie.

Der Wahrsager lacht. „Machen Sie weiter, und Sie werden sehr erfolgreich sein. Sie werden mit Kunst viel Geld verdienen! Sind Sie in der jüngeren Vergangenheit auf einige Hindernisse gestoßen? Wie Probleme mit der Arbeit und auf Reisen?"

Rose ist sehr überrascht, diese Frage zu hören, und Jack ist auch ein wenig schockiert.

"Ja! Es begann mit einem Bahnstreik und hat seitdem nicht nachgelassen. Der Grund, warum wir hier sind, ist, dass unser Taxi eine Panne hatte.", sagt Rose.

„Ich werde das Problem für Sie lösen."

Der Wahrsager holt drei kleine Kristallfächer aus

einem Schrank in der Nähe. Er legt die Kristallkugel auf den Tisch und rezitiert etwas.

„Oh, Kristallkugel, nimm alle Probleme dieses Mädchens und dieses Mannes weg! Bring sie sicher nach Hause!", sagt der Wahrsager und stellt seinen Fächer daneben. Er signalisiert Jack und Rose ebenfalls, **ihre** zu platzieren, und sie tun dies. Jack ist etwas zögerlich und misstrauisch, aber Rose ist sehr beeindruckt und aufgeregt. Er fährt fort, die nächsten paar Minuten Mantras zu rezitieren. Jack spürt, dass etwas nicht stimmt und signalisiert Rose dies. Rose stimmt nicht zu. Sie fragt stattdessen:

„Können Sie etwas über mein Liebesleben vorhersagen?"

"Ja, natürlich! Was möchten Sie wissen?"

„Wann treffe ich meinen Partner fürs Leben?", fragt Rose und errötet.

Der Mann beobachtet etwas auf ihrer Handfläche und auf dem Papier. „Sie kennen **ihn** schon!", sagt er.

"Was?!", ruft Rose.

"Ja. Sie sind ihm bereits begegnet."

"Wirklich? Wer kann das sein?", wundert sich Rose.

„Er ist der Mann, der neben Ihnen sitzt!", sagt der Wahrsager.

Jack steht überrascht von seinem Stuhl auf. „Was sagen Sie da? Ich bin in jemand anderen verliebt!", sagt Jack.

Rose errötet. Sie freut sich sehr über die Vorhersage Wahrsagers.

„Sie werden diese Frau heiraten! Merken Sie sich meine Worte."

Jack weiß nicht, wie er reagieren soll. Er ist überrascht über das Selbstbewusstsein des Wahrsagers.

„So viele Paare sind zu mir zurückgekommen und haben gesagt, dass sich meine Vorhersage bewahrheitet hat!", sagt der Wahrsager. „Alle Hindernisse, mit denen Sie bisher in Bezug auf Ihre Reise konfrontiert waren, werden bald überwunden sein."

"Vielen, vielen Dank! Sie sind wirklich bemerkenswert!", sagt Rose.

„Zeigen Sie **mir** Ihre Handfläche, junger Mann. Lassen Sie mich Ihnen sagen, was Ihre Zukunft bringt", sagt der Wahrsager zu Jack.

„Sie haben bereits etwas Unverschämtes gesagt! Ich bin schockiert!", sagt Jack und streckt **seine** Hand aus.

„Haben Sie spezielle Fragen?"

"Nicht wirklich! Eigentlich fällt mir nichts ein", sagt Jack.

"Macht nichts! Ich werde Ihnen einen allgemeinen Überblick geben", sagt der Wahrsager und beginnt, etwas auf das Papier zu zeichnen, ähnlich wie er es für Roses Handfläche getan hat. Er sagt Jack eine glänzende Zukunft voraus. Rose stellt dem Wahrsager einige weitere Fragen über ihr Leben und die beiden verbringen eine halbe Stunde dort, bevor Jack den Wahrsager bezahlt.

"Vielen Dank! Es war sehr nett, Sie zu kennen zu lernen! Sie haben einige wirklich gute und unglaubliche Dinge über meine Zukunft vorhergesagt! Ich werde mich auf jeden Fall bei Ihnen melden, falls ich diese zierliche Frau heiraten sollte", sagt Jack lächelnd.

Der Wahrsager lacht herzlich und sagt: „Ihr werdet ein glückliches Leben zusammen haben! All meinen Segen für Sie beide! Alles Gute! **Ihre** ist eine der besten Handflächen, die ich bisher gesehen habe."

„Ich weiß nicht, was **es** mit meiner Handfläche auf sich hat, aber ich bin mir sicher, dass **unsere** Freundschaft die beste aller Zeiten sein wird", sagt Rose.

Jack und Rose danken dem Wahrsager und gehen.

SUMMARY

Der Fahrer bringt Jack und Rose zum Haus des Wahrsagers. Rose geht unterwegs der Schuh kaputt, sie schafft es aber trotzdem, bis zum Ziel zu laufen. Der Fahrer stellt sie dem Wahrsager vor und geht. Der Wahrsager untersucht die Handflächen von Jack und Rose und macht eine Reihe von Vorhersagen über ihre jeweilige Zukunft. Die unglaublichste Vorhersage von allen ist, dass Jack und Rose heiraten werden. Diese Vorhersage schockiert Jack.

WORDS TO REMEMBER

1. **Ihr** - Their
2. **Vor ihnen** – In front of them
3. **Sie** - They
4. **Sie** - Her
5. **Seine** - His
6. **Du** - You
7. **Dein** - Your
8. **Ich** - I
9. **Mein** - My
10. **Mir** - Me
11. **Wir** - We
12. **Meine** - Mine
13. **Unser** - Our
14. **Sie** - She
15. **Es** - It
16. **Deine** - Yours
17. **Er** - He

18. **Es ist** – It is
19. **Ihre** - Theirs
20. **Ihn** - Him
21. **Ihres** - Hers
22. **Unsere** - Ours

QUESTIONS

1. Welches Problem hat Rose auf dem Weg zum Haus des Wahrsagers?

- a. Sie tut sich weh
- b. Sie hat einen Unfall
- c. Ihr Schuh geht kaputt
- d. Sie verliert ihre Tasche

2. Welche der folgenden Aussagen trifft auf das Haus des Wahrsagers zu?

- a. Es ist kaputt
- b. Es ist rot
- c. Es ist aus Marmor
- d. Es ist das größte Haus in der Gasse

3. Wie fühlt sich Jack, als er das Haus zum ersten Mal betritt?

- a. Er fühlt sich sehr glücklich

- b. Er fühlt sich nicht wohl
- c. Er ist sehr beeindruckt
- d. Er ist sehr aufgeregt

4. Welche ist die schockierendste Vorhersage des Wahrsagers?

- a. Jack und Rose werden heiraten
- b. Jack wird der reichste Mann der Welt
- c. Rose wird eine Berühmtheit
- d. Rose und Jack werden zu Feinden

5. Worüber neckt Jack Rose?

- a. Ihr Gewicht
- b. Ihr Kleid
- c. Ihre Nase
- d. Ihre Schuhgröße

―――――

ANSWERS

1. **c.** Ihr Schuh geht kaputt
2. **d.** Es ist das größte Haus in der Gasse
3. **b.** Er fühlt sich nicht wohl
4. **a.** Jack und Rose werden heiraten
5. **d.** Ihre Schuhgröße

ENGLISH TRANSLATION

The weather is pleasant, the sun is about to set, and the road is quiet. Jack, Rose, and the driver are walking towards the house of the fortune-teller. The sound of their footsteps is echoing. The driver walks briskly in front of the two of them. He appears to be very fit. Jack can catch up to his speed, but Rose is cannot. One of her shoes is broken.

"How are you going to walk in these shoes? Your other shoe will also break very soon," Jack says laughing.

"Shush! Don't say that, Jack! If my other shoe breaks, I will be in serious trouble," Rose says.

"What's your shoe size?" Jack says, looking at her tiny feet.

"Mine? I know, it's quite small," Rose says smiling.

"There was a very nice store on the outskirts of that village that we were in. They also had a good collection of shoes, but there was no kids section in that store!" Jack remarks laughing.

"You are making fun of me! I am the tallest girl in our family," Rose says smiling.

"Wow! Congratulations!" says Jack.

She laughs.

"We will now go down this lane on the left. It is a bit rocky, but it's the shortest route," the driver says.

"All the best to you and yours for the journey ahead!" Jack says smiling at Rose.

"My shoes are doing a great job until now! I will manage," says Rose, but he is doubtful.

"Your other shoe doesn't seem to be in good condition. I think its sole is coming out on one side," he says.

"No, it's fine. I'll make it to the fortune-teller's house," she says.

The road is very narrow now and the three of them continue to walk. There are a few houses spread far apart, and the driver points at the last one. The house is not too large, but it's the largest one on that lane. The door is open slightly, and through it, you can see a crystal ball. The driver knocks on the door and calls out,

"Mr. Burgundy! It's me, Paul."

"Oh, hello, Paul! Please come in." the fortune-teller replies.

"You have two visitors. I have brought them with me."

Jack and Rose hear the sound of a chair being dragged on the floor and then footsteps. Mr. Burgundy comes to the door. He greets Jack and Rose and they follow him inside. Jack doesn't like the place. He is uncomfortable, but he says nothing. The fortuneteller takes them into a room where there is a table and chairs.

"Please have a seat," says the fortune-teller.

"You enjoy this session, now. I will wait in the car. The mechanic will be here soon," the driver says and leaves.

Jack and Rose sit down and the fortuneteller sits opposite them.

"Ok, so who would like to start?" the man asks.

"Me!" Rose immediately responds.

The fortune-teller laughs and asks her to present her hand.

"So you are a palmist. Don't you use a crystal ball?" Jack asks.

Rose is confused. She knows nothing about palmistry or crystal balls.

"Yes! I use both," says the fortune-teller.

Rose extends her palm and says, "I am ready."

The fortune-teller carefully examines her palm and the

various lines on it. He draws out something on a piece of paper.

"You are a very fortunate girl! You are very artistic. Do you work in the art field?" he asks.

Rose is very impressed. "Yes, absolutely!" she says.

The fortune-teller laughs. "Just continue, and you will be very successful. You will make a lot of money with art! Did you face some obstacles in the recent past? Like problems with work and travel?"

Rose is very surprised to hear this question, and Jack is a little shocked too.

"Yes! It started with a train strike and hasn't let up since. The reason we are here is that our cab broke down." Rose says.

"I will solve the problem for you."

The fortune-teller fetches three little crystal fans from a cupboard nearby. He places the crystal ball on the table and recites something.

"Oh, crystal ball, take away all the problems of this girl and this man! Take them home safely!" the fortune-teller says and places his fan near it. He signals Jack and Rose also to place theirs, and they do so. Jack is a bit hesitant and suspicious, but Rose is very impressed and excited. He continues to recite some mantras for the next few minutes. Jack feels that something is not right and he signals this to Rose. Rose doesn't agree. She instead asks,

"Can you predict something about my love life?"

"Yes, of course! What do you want to know?"

"When will I meet my life partner?" Rose asks with a blush.

The man observes something on her palm and on the paper. "You already know him!" he says.

"What?!" exclaims Rose.

"Yes. You have met him."

"Really! Who can that be?" Rose wonders.

"He's the man sitting next to you!" says the fortune-teller.

Jack stands up from his chair in surprise. "What are you saying, sir? I'm in love with someone else!" Jack says.

Rose blushes. She feels very happy to hear the fortune-teller's prediction.

"You will marry this woman! Mark my words."

Jack doesn't know how to react. He's surprised at the fortune-teller's confidence.

"So many couples have come back to me saying that my prediction has come true!" says the fortune-teller. "All the obstacles you were facing until now with regard to your travel will be over soon."

"Thank you so much, sir! You are really amazing!" Rose says.

"Show me your palm, gentleman. Let me tell you what your future holds," the fortune-teller tells Jack.

"You have already said an outrageous thing! I am shocked!" Jack says and extends his hand.

"Do you have any particular questions?"

"Not really! Actually, I am unable to think of anything," Jack says.

"Never mind! I will give you a general overview," the fortune-teller says and begins drawing something on the paper, similarly to what he did for Rose's palm. He predicts a very bright future for Jack. Rose asks the fortuneteller some more questions about her life, and the two of them spend half an hour there before Jack pays the fortune-teller.

"Thank you very much, sir! It was very nice meeting you! You have predicted some really good and unbelievable things for my future! I will definitely get in touch with you in case I happen to marry this petite woman." Jack says, smiling.

The fortune-teller laughs heartily and says, "You will have a happy life together! All my blessings to you both! All the best! Hers is one of the best palms I have ever seen so far."

"I don't know about my palm, or ours, but I'm sure ours is going to be the best friendship ever," Rose says.

Jack and Rose thank the fortune-teller and leave.

3
THE HOTEL
COMMON EVERYDAY OBJECTS

Jack und Rose sind auf dem Weg zurück zum Auto. Jack schaut auf sein **Handy**, es ist 19 Uhr. Die Worte des Wahrsagers über die Heirat mit Rose sind ihm immer noch in Erinnerung. Rose denkt über dasselbe nach. Vor Freude schwingt sie ihre **Handtasche** in der Hand, als sie mit ihren kaputten **Schuhen** über den steinigen Weg geht. Sie sagen nichts zueinander. Sie erreichen die Hauptstraße und finden dort den Fahrer und den Mechaniker.

„Was ist mit dem Auto los?", fragt Jack den Fahrer.

"Oh Hallo. Sie sind zurück!", sagt der Fahrer und setzt seine **Brille** auf. „Der Mechaniker hat den Motor überprüft. Er denkt, dass er das Auto in seine Werkstatt bringen muss, um das Problem zu beheben."

"OK. Also lasst uns unsere **Koffer** aus dem Auto ausladen", sagt Jack und steckt seine **Geldbörse** in die Tasche seiner **Jeans**.

„Warte, Jack! Ich werde dir helfen!", sagt Rose, geht langsam auf ihn zu und schleift ihre Schuhe über den Boden.

„Fräulein Zierlich, danke. Du kümmerst dich um dich selbst, ich kümmere mich um deine Tasche", sagt Jack.

„Willst du dich nicht um mich kümmern?", flüstert sie.

"Entschuldige? Das habe ich nicht gehört", sagt Jack.

"Nichts! Ich sagte: 'Gib mir deinen **Stift**, ich werde ihn halten.'"

"Wirklich?!"

"Na sicher!", sagt sie selbstbewusst.

„Fräulein Zierlich, ich habe keinen Stift in der Hand. Tatsächlich hat mein **Hemd** nicht einmal eine Tasche, um einen Stift darin aufzubewahren. Überlege dir eine Antwort, während ich die Koffer auslade", sagt Jack und geht weg.

Rose ist verlegen. Sie steht lächelnd da und sagt nichts.

„Können Sie uns mit dem Auto des Mechanikers am Hotel absetzen?", fragt Jack den Fahrer.

„Oh ja, auf jeden Fall! Lassen Sie mich die Schlüssel von ihm holen!", antwortet der Fahrer und geht, um die Schlüssel vom Mechaniker zu holen.

Jack sieht Rose an und sie erwidert seinen Blick.

„Lass mich kurz mein Gesicht und meine Haare überprüfen, bevor wir gehen", sagt sie und öffnet ihre Handtasche.

Sie nimmt zuerst einen **Kamm** und fährt damit durch ihr glänzendes schwarzes Haar. Dann holt sie einen Spiegel heraus und überprüft ihr Haar darin. Sie rundet ihren Look schließlich ab, indem sie ihre Lieblings**lotion** und einen rosa **Lippenstift** anwendet und das Ganze mit einem großzügigen Sprüher ihres **Parfüms** vervollständigt.

"Ich bin soweit!", sagt Rose und packt all ihre Sachen zurück in ihre Handtasche.

„Hast du ein zusätzliches Paar Schuhe?", fragt Jack, während er ihre kaputten Schuhe betrachtet.

"Nein. Ich hatte nicht damit gerechnet, dass so etwas passiert."

„Sind wir bereit, zum Hotel zu fahren?", fragt der Fahrer aus dem Auto des Mechanikers.

Jack und Rose steigen ins Auto und der Fahrer fährt los. In etwa zehn Minuten erreichen sie das Hotel. Das Hotel ist ein kleines Gebäude in der Nähe des Waldes. Jack und Rose steigen aus dem Auto, laden ihre Taschen aus, danken dem Fahrer und gehen hinein.

„Guten Abend, mein Herr; guten Abend, meine Dame! Herzlich willkommen!", sagt der Rezeptionist.

"Hallo!", sagt Jack. „Wir möchten hier zwei Zimmer für die Nacht reservieren", fügt er hinzu.

"Selbstverständlich. Bitte setzen sie sich", antwortet der Mann.

Er tippt etwas in den **Computer** ein und wählt dann eine Nummer am **Telefon**. Er spricht ca. 5 Minuten mit seinem Kollegen auf der anderen Seite und legt dann auf.

„Wir haben nur ein Einzelzimmer frei. Sind Sie damit einverstanden?", sagt der Mann.

"Gar nicht!", antwortet Jack.

"In Ordnung. Dann gibt es noch eine andere Möglichkeit. Wir haben eine Suite mit zwei Schlafzimmern. Möchten Sie das nehmen?"

"Das ist besser. Wie viel kostet es pro Nacht?", fragt Jack.

„Wie lange möchten Sie bei uns bleiben?", fragt der Mann und kritzelt mit seinem **Bleistift** etwas auf seinen **Notizblock**.

„Zwei Nächte."

Er zückt seinen Taschenrechner und gibt ein paar

Zahlen ein. „Das wären 120 Euro pro Nacht, inklusive aller Steuern."

„Bitte erlaube mir, für eine Nacht zu bezahlen, Jack", unterbricht Rose.

Jack stimmt zu und die Zahlungen werden geleistet. Der Mann übergibt Jack die Zimmerschlüssel und gibt ihm auch ein **Buch** mit Details über alle Annehmlichkeiten des Hotels.

„Bei Ihrem Aufenthalt ist das Frühstück für beide Nächte inbegriffen. Wir organisieren auch Tagesausflüge für unsere Gäste zu einigen beliebten Touristenorten in der Nähe. Wenn Sie einen Ausflug planen wollen, können Sie sich gerne mit mir in Verbindung setzen. Genießen Sie Ihren Aufenthalt bei uns", sagt der Mann.

"Sicher. Vielen Dank!", sagt Jack und die beiden gehen auf ihr Zimmer.

„Es ist ein schönes Zimmer!", sagt Rose.

„Ja, ziemlich gut für diesen Ort", antwortet Jack.

„Sollen wir jetzt essen gehen? Dann können wir planen, was wir morgen unternehmen wollen," schlägt Rose vor.

„Die Tagesausflüge, von denen der Mann an der Rezeption gesprochen hat, klingen ganz nett. Wir können morgen einen in den Wald unternehmen."

"Großartige Idee! Ich freue mich darauf, den Wald zu besuchen", sagt Rose und macht einen kleinen Tanz.

„Mach nicht den Fehler zu denken, dass ich dich auffangen werde, wenn deine Schuhe versagen und du hinfällst", scherzt Jack.

„Ich weiß, was für ein Gentleman du bist, und du bist auch mein Freund. Ich bin mir sicher, dass du mich auffangen wirst."

Es klingelt an der Tür und Jack geht, um zu sehen, wer da ist.

"Guten Abend! Hier sind Ihre Taschen", sagt der Mann auf der anderen Seite.

Jack lässt ihn ein. Der Mann arrangiert beide Taschen auf der Gepäckablage und sagt: „Bitte gestatten Sie mir einen Moment, um Ihnen alles zu zeigen, was dieses Zimmer zu bieten hat."

„Ja, bitte fahren Sie fort", sagt Jack.

"Danke", sagt der Mann und erzählt den beiden vom Fernseher, der **Lautsprechern**, der **Stereoanlage**, der Minibar und den Möglichkeiten, im Zimmer zu speisen.

„Gibt es irgendwelche Möglichkeiten, **Kleidung** oder Schuhe für den Waldausflug zu leihen?", fragt Rose.

„Leider nicht. Sie können eine **Kamera** für einen Tag ausleihen, wenn Sie möchten. Ein Set mit einigen grundlegenden Erste-Hilfe-Artikeln, einer **Schere**, einigen gängigen **Medikamenten** und einer Taschenlampe ist in jedem Tagestourpaket enthalten und wird Ihnen zum Zeitpunkt der Buchung ausgehändigt", sagt der Mann.

"OK. Danke", sagt Rose.

Der Mann geht.

„Ich werde mich schnell fürs Abendessen schick machen", sagt Rose und holt ihr **Make-up**-Set aus ihrer Tasche.

„Schnell, Fräulein Zierlich!", sagt Jack und stellt seinen **Laptop** auf den Tisch.

„Ich kann den **Mülleimer** in diesem Zimmer nicht finden, Jack. Wo ist er?", fragt Rose.

"Er ist genau dort, wo deine wunderschön kaputten Schuhe sind", scherzt Jack.

„Das kann nicht dein Ernst sein!", sagt Rose und wirft ihre **Bürste** nach Jack. Jack lächelt.

SUMMARY

Jack und Rose kommen im Hotel an und beziehen eine Suite für das Wochenende. Das Hotelpersonal stellt ihnen alle verfügbaren Annehmlichkeiten und Tourpakete vor. Zwischen den beiden entwickelt sich eine freundschaftliche und scherzhafte Bindung.

WORDS TO REMEMBER

1. **Handy** - Mobile phone
2. **Schuhe** - Shoes
3. **Handtasche** - Handbag
4. **Brille** - Glasses
5. **Koffer** - Suitcases
6. **Geldbörse** - Wallet
7. **Jeans** - Jeans
8. **Stift** - Pen
9. **Hemd** - Shirt
10. **Kamm** - Comb
11. **Lippenstift** - Lipstick
12. **Parfüm** - Perfume
13. **Lotion** - Lotion
14. **Telefon** - Telephone
15. **Computer** - Computer
16. **Bleistift** - Pencil
17. **Notizblock** - Notepad
18. **Buch** - Book
19. **Stereoanlage** - Stereoanlage
20. **Lautsprecher** - Speaker
21. **Medikamente** - Medicines

22. **Kleidung** - Clothes
23. **Kamera** - Camera
24. **Schere** - Scissors
25. **Laptop** - Laptop
26. **Make-up** – Make up
27. **Bürste** - Brush
28. **Mülleimer** - Garbage

QUESTIONS

1. Was für ein Zimmer buchen Jack und Rose für ihren Aufenthalt im Hotel?

- a. Ein Deluxe-Zimmer
- b. Ein Standardzimmer
- c. Ein Executive-Zimmer
- d. Eine Suite

2. Was gibt der Rezeptionist Jack zusammen mit den Schlüsseln?

- a. Ein Buch
- b. Eine Karte
- c. Einen Stift
- d. Einen Rabattgutschein

3. Welche der folgenden Aussagen ist richtig?

- a. Die Suite hat fünf Zimmer
- b. Die Suite ist für Jack und Rose kostenlos
- c. Die Suite ist nicht verfügbar
- d. Die Suite verfügt über eine Minibar

4. Was macht Rose, nachdem sie ins Zimmer gegangen ist?

- a. Sie macht sich schick für das Abendessen
- b. Sie ruft ihre Mutter an
- c. Sie duscht
- d. Sie geht ins Bett

5. Was kann Rose im Zimmer nicht finden?

- a. Den Fernseher
- b. Den Mülleimer
- c. Die Minibar
- d. Das Sofa

ANSWERS

1. **d.** Eine Suite
2. **a.** Ein Buch
3. **d.** Die Suite verfügt über eine Minibar
4. **a.** Sie macht sich schick für das Abendessen
5. **b.** Den Mülleimer

ENGLISH TRANSLATION

Jack and Rose are on their way back to the car. Jack checks his mobile phone, and the time is 7 p.m. The words of the fortune-teller about marrying Rose are still on his mind. Rose is thinking about the same thing. She swings her handbag in her hand in joy as she makes her way across the rocky lane in her broken shoes. They say nothing to one another. They reach the main road and find the driver and the mechanic there.

"What's wrong with the car?" Jack asks the driver.

"Oh, hello. sir! You're back!" the driver says and puts on his glasses. "The mechanic has checked the engine. He feels he will have to take the car to his shop to fix the issue."

"Ok. So, let's unload our suitcases from the car then." Jack says and slips his wallet into the pocket of his jeans.

"Wait, Jack! I'll help you!" Rose says and walks slowly towards him dragging her shoes on the ground.

"Miss Petite, thank you. You handle yourself, I will handle your bag." Jack says.

"Will you not handle me?" she whispers.

"Sorry? I didn't hear that," says Jack.

"Nothing! I said, "Give me your pen, I will hold it."

"Really?!"

"Of course!" she says confidently.

"Miss Petite, I don't have a pen in my hand. In fact, my shirt doesn't even have a pocket to hold one. Think of a reply while I unload the suitcases." Jack says and goes away.

Rose is embarrassed. She stands up there smiling and says nothing.

"Will you be able to drop us at the hotel in the mechanic's car?" Jack asks the driver.

"Oh, yes, definitely! Let me get the keys from him!" the driver replies and goes to fetch the keys from the mechanic.

Jack looks at Rose and she looks back.

"Let me just check my face and hair before we leave," she says and opens her handbag.

She first takes out a comb and runs it through her shiny black hair. She then pulls out a mirror and checks her hair in it. She finally finishes her look with an application of her favorite lotion, a pink lipstick, and a generous spraying of perfume.

"I am ready to go!" Rose says putting all her belongings back into her handbag.

"Do you have an additional pair of shoes?" Jack asks while looking at her broken ones.

"No. I never imagined this happening."

"Are we ready to go to the hotel?" the driver asks from inside the mechanic's car.

Jack and Rose get into the car, and the driver takes them away. In about ten minutes, they arrive at the hotel. The hotel is a small building near the forest. Jack and Rose get out of the car, unload their bags, thank the driver, and walk in.

"Good evening, sir, good evening, madam! Welcome!" says the receptionist.

"Hello!" says Jack. "We would like to reserve two rooms here for the night," he adds.

"Sure sir. Please take a seat." replies the man.

He types something on the computer and then dials a number on the telephone. He speaks to his colleague on the other side for about five minutes and then hangs up.

"We only have one single room available, sir. Are you okay with that?" says the man.

"Not at all!" Jack replies.

"All right. So, then there is another option. We have a two-bedroom suite. Would you like to take that?"

"That's better. How much does it cost per night?" Jack asks.

"For how long would you like to stay with us?" the man asks and scribbles something on his notepad with his pencil.

"Tonight and tomorrow night."

He pulls out his calculator and puts in some numbers. "That will be €120 per night, inclusive of all taxes."

"Please allow me to pay for one night, Jack." Rose interrupts.

Jack agrees and the payments are made. The man hands over the keys to the room to Jack and also gives him a book containing details about all the amenities of the hotel.

"You have breakfast included with your stay for both nights sir. We also organize day tours for our guests to some popular tourist locations nearby. If you need to plan one, please feel free to get in touch with me. Enjoy your stay with us." says the man.

"Sure. Thank you!" Jack says and the two of them go to their room.

"It's a nice room!" says Rose.

"Yeah, quite good for this place," Jack replies.

"Shall we go for dinner now? Then we can plan what to do tomorrow." Rose suggests.

"The day tours the man at the desk was talking about sound quite nice. We can take one to the forest tomorrow."

"Great idea! I am excited to visit the forest." Rose says, doing a little dance.

"Don't make the mistake of thinking that I will hold you if your shoes fail you and you fall down." Jack jokes.

"I know what a gentleman you are and you are also my friend. I am certain you will hold me."

The doorbell rings and Jack goes to check the door.

"Good evening, sir! Here are your bags." says the man on the other side.

Jack lets him in. The man arranges both bags on the luggage rack and says, "Please allow me a moment to introduce you to all the facilities that are available in this room."

"Yes, please go ahead," Jack says.

"Thank you, sir." the man says and tells the two of them about the TV set, the speaker and stereo system, the minibar, and the in-room dining options.

"Do you have any product rental facilities like clothes or shoes for the forest trip?" Rose asks.

"No, madam. You can rent a camera for a day if you please. A kit containing some basic first aid items, a pair of scissors, some common medicines, and a torch is included with every day tour package and will be given to you at the time of booking." says the man.

"Ok. Thank you," says Rose.

The man leaves.

"I will quickly dress up for dinner," Rose says and removes her makeup kit from her bag.

"Fast, Miss Petite!" Jack says and places his laptop on the table.

"I can't find the garbage bin in this room, Jack, where is it?" Rose asks.

"It's right where your beautiful, broken shoes are." Jack jokes.

"You can't be serious!" Rose says and throws her brush at Jack. Jack smiles.

4
SATURDAY
NUMBERS

Jack und Rose wachen am nächsten Morgen früh auf und machen sich bereit, in den Wald aufzubrechen. Es gibt **fünfzehn** Zimmer auf ihrer Etage und ihres ist dem Aufzug am nächsten.

„Was meinst du, wie viele Zimmer dieses Hotel insgesamt hat?", fragt Rose, als sie die Tür ihres Zimmers schließen und den Flur hinuntergehen.

„Dieses Hotel hat **zwei** Stockwerke. Wenn beide Stockwerke die gleiche Anzahl an Zimmern haben, müssten es **dreißig** sein", antwortet Jack.

„Ich glaube, sie haben auch Zimmer im Erdgeschoss."

"Tatsächlich?"

"Ja. Ich habe dort **fünf** Zimmer gesehen, als wir gestern Abend zum Abendessen gingen. Das macht also **fünfunddreißig** Zimmer", sagt Rose.

„Nicht schlecht, Fräulein Zierlich! Du bist gut in Mathe!", neckt Jack.

Der Fahrstuhl kommt und sie steigen ein. Darin befinden sich bereits zwei Männer und **drei** Frauen. Jack fühlt sich unwohl wegen der vielen Menschen im Aufzug, aber er sagt nichts.

Als sie das Erdgeschoss erreichen, gehen alle schnell hinaus. Jack und Rose gehen zur Rezeption. Dort sind **vier** Männer, aber die Person, mit der sie letzte Nacht gesprochen haben, ist nicht zu finden.

„Wie kann ich Ihnen helfen?", fragt **ein** Mann Jack.

„Wir haben für heute die Tagestour durch den Wald gebucht", sagt Jack.

"Gut. Die Tour beginnt um **sechs**, in **fünfundzwanzig** Minuten. Bitte nehmen Sie Platz und ich werde Sie informieren, sobald der Tourbus ankommt", sagt der Mann.

"Sicher! Vielen Dank", sagt Jack.

"Was ist Ihre Zimmernummer?", fragt der Mann.

"**Dreizehn**."

„Und haben Sie irgendwelche Taschen?"

„Nur eine Handtasche."

"OK", sagt der Mann und notiert die Details.

Jack und Rose setzen sich auf die bequem gepolsterten Sofas in der Lobby. Die Lobby ist klein und gemütlich. Es ist weitgehend leer. Die **sieben** Personen, die mit Jack und Rose im Fahrstuhl waren, sind nirgendwo zu sehen. Nach etwa **zwanzig** Minuten kommt **ein** Reisebus an. Es ist ein **Zwölf**sitzer. Der Mann an der Rezeption informiert Jack und Rose, dass sie in den Bus einsteigen können.

„Wenn Sie möchten, können Sie im Bus Platz nehmen", sagt der Mann.

"Wann fährt der Bus ab?", fragt Rose.

„In genau **achtzehn** Minuten", sagt der Mann. „Aufgrund einiger technischer Probleme im Fahrzeug gab es eine kleine Verzögerung. Ab diesem Hotel nehmen sieben weitere Personen an der Tour teil. Sobald sie ankommen, fährt der Bus ab."

"Gut!", sagt Rose.

Die Zeit vergeht und der Bus füllt sich. Die Reise

beginnt zum richtigen Zeitpunkt. Der Bus erreicht bald den Wald. Alle Passagiere steigen aus und der Reiseleiter sagt:

„Achtung, meine Damen und Herren! Wir werden jetzt unsere Wanderung beginnen. Bitte bleiben Sie bei der Gruppe und zögern Sie nicht, auf mich zuzukommen, wenn Sie irgendetwas brauchen."

Der Reiseleiter verteilt Landkarten an alle Touristen und alle machen sich auf den Weg. Es gibt über **tausend** Baumarten und **hundert** verschiedene Tier- und Vogelarten im Wald. Jack und Rose genießen die Schönheit der Natur.

„Dieser Ort ist so ruhig, nicht wahr?", sagt Jack.
"Ja, ist es. Darf ich dich etwas fragen?", sagt Rose.
"Ja."
„Was hast du gedacht, als der Wahrsager sagte, dass wir heiraten werden?"
"Unmöglich!"
„Hast du das wirklich gedacht?"
"Ja. Schau, Rose, bitte baue keine Hoffnungen oder Träume aufgrund dessen, was er gesagt hat. Ich liebe jemand anderes", sagt Jack.
Rose sagt nichts.
„Es tut mir leid, Rose", sagt Jack.
Sie sagt nichts und verschwindet hinter den Bäumen.
"Wo gehst du hin?", ruft Jack.
"Warte dort! Ich komme!", sagt Rose.
Sie kommt **zehn** Minuten später mit **fünfzig** Rosen in der Hand zurück.

„Jack, ich weiß nicht, was du über mich denkst. Ich weiß nicht, ob du mich jemals lieben wirst, aber es ist mir egal. Ich weiß nur, dass du mir die Welt bedeutest. Ich liebe dich, Jack, und das werde ich für den Rest meines Lebens tun. Du bist nicht gezwungen, mich zurück zu lieben. Meine Worte mögen dir unwirklich erscheinen, aber meine Gefühle für dich sind absolut rein und wahr", sagt Rose.

Alle anderen Mitglieder der Wandergruppe klatschen in die Hände und jubeln. Jack ist völlig sprachlos.

„Ich weiß es wirklich zu schätzen, was du für mich empfindest, Rose. Ich danke dir sehr! Du wirst immer etwas Besonderes für mich sein", sagt Jack und umarmt Rose. Die Wanderung geht zu Ende und alle Touristen, einschließlich Jack und Rose, kehren zum Hotel zurück. Jack kann sich mit Roses Geständnis nicht abfinden. Sie tut ihm leid. Kathryns Gesicht erscheint vor seinen Augen.

„Bitte vergib mir, Rose! Mein Herz schlägt nur für Kathryn", denkt Jack bei sich.

SUMMARY

Jack und Rose machen sich zusammen mit einer Gruppe anderer Leute auf den Weg in den Wald. Sie genießen die Natur und die Tierwelt. Rose bringt dann ihre Gefühle für Jack zum Ausdruck. Jack lehnt sie höflich ab, weil er Kathryn liebt. Er betrachtet Rose als eine besondere Freundin.

WORDS TO REMEMBER

1. **Fünfzehn** - Fifteen

2. **Dreißig** - Thirty
3. **Fünf** - Five
4. **Fünfunddreißig** - Thirty-five
5. **Zwei** - Two
6. **Drei** - Three
7. **Vier** - Four
8. **Sechs** - Six
9. **Fünfundzwanzig** - Twenty-five
10. **Dreizehn** - Thirteen
11. **Zehn** - Ten
12. **Eins** - One
13. **Zwanzig** - Twenty
14. **Zwölf** - Twelve
15. **Achtzehn** - Eighteen
16. **Sieben** - Seven
17. **Hundert** - Hundred
18. **Tausend** - Thousand
19. **Fünfzig** - Fifty

———

QUESTIONS

1. Wie viele Zimmer gibt es in dem Hotel, in dem Jack und Rose übernachten?

- a. Sechs
- b. Siebenundzwanzig
- c. Zweiunddreißig
- d. Fünfunddreißig

2. Wie viele Personen reisen von ihrem Hotel aus im Bus mit Jack und Rose?

- a. Fünf
- b. Sieben
- c. Neun
- d. Elf

3. Was gibt der Reiseleiter allen Touristen vor der Wanderung mit?

- a. Eine Landkarte
- b. Einen Regenschirm
- c. Einen Korb
- d. Ein Paar Schuhe

4. Was gibt Rose Jack im Wald?

- a. Ein Stück Kuchen
- b. Eine Schachtel Pralinen
- c. Fünfzig Rosen
- d. Ein Eis

5. Was erzählt Rose Jack über ihre Gefühle?

- a. Ich liebe dich, und das werde ich für den Rest meines Lebens tun.
- b. Ich hasse dich jetzt und für immer

- c. Du bist mein bester Freund
- d. Ich mag dein Lächeln

ANSWERS

1. **d.** Fünfunddreißig
2. **b.** Sieben
3. **a.** Eine Landkarte
4. **c.** Fünfzig Rosen
5. **a.** Ich liebe dich, und das werde ich für den Rest meines Lebens tun

---

ENGLISH TRANSLATION

Jack and Rose wake up early the next morning and get ready to leave for the forest. There are fifteen rooms on their floor and theirs is the closest to the elevator.

"How many rooms do you think this hotel has in total?" Rose asks as they shut the door of their room and walk down the hallway.

"This hotel has two floors. If both floors have the same number of rooms, there must be thirty," Jack replies.

"I think they also have rooms on the ground floor."

"Do they?"

"Yes. I saw five of them when we went down for dinner last evening. So that makes it thirty-five rooms," says Rose.

"Not bad, Miss Petite! You are good at math!" Jack teases.

The elevator arrives and they get on. There are already

two men and three women in there. Jack is uncomfortable about the large number of people in the elevator, but he says nothing.

As they reach the ground floor, everyone exits rapidly. Jack and Rose walk to the front desk. There are four men there but the person they spoke to last night is not to be found.

"How may I help you, sir?" one man asks Jack.

"We have a booking for the forest day tour today," Jack says.

"All right. The tour departs at six, twenty-five minutes from now. Please have a seat and I will let you know once the tour bus arrives," the man says.

"Sure! Thank you." Jack says.

"What is your room number?" the man asks.

"Thirteen."

"And do you have any bags?"

"Just one handbag."

"Ok." the man says and notes down the details.

Jack and Rose sit down on the comfortable cushioned sofas in the lobby. The lobby is small and cozy. It is largely empty. The seven people who were with Jack and Rose in the elevator are not to be seen anywhere. After about twenty minutes, a tour bus arrives. It is a twelve-seater. The man at the front desk informs Jack and Rose that they can board the bus.

"You may go and take your seats in the bus if you like," says the man.

"When will the bus depart?" Rose asks.

"In precisely eighteen minutes." the man says. "There was a bit of a delay because of some technical issues in the vehicle. There are seven more people joining the tour from this hotel. As soon as they arrive, the bus will leave."

"All right!" says Rose.

Time passes by and the bus fills up. The journey begins at the right time. The bus soon reaches the forest. All the passengers disembark, and the tour guide says,

"Attention, ladies and gentlemen! We will now begin our trek. Please stay with the group and don't hesitate to come to me if you need anything."

The tour guide hands out a map to all the tourists and everyone starts walking. There are over a thousand varieties of trees and a hundred different species of animals and birds in the forest. Jack and Rose enjoy the beauty of nature.

"This place is so tranquil, isn't it?" says Jack.

"Yeah, it is. Can I ask you something?" says Rose.

"Yes."

"What did you think when the fortune-teller said that we'll end up married?"

"Impossible!"

"Is this what you really thought?"

"Yes. Look, Rose, don't build any hopes or dreams around what he said. I love someone else." Jack says.

Rose says nothing.

"I am sorry, Rose," Jack says.

She says nothing and disappears behind the trees.

"Where are you going?" Jack calls out.

"Wait there! I am coming!" Rose says.

She returns in ten minutes with fifty roses in her hand.

"Jack, I don't know what you think about me. I don't know if you will ever love me but I don't care. All I know is that you mean the world to me. I love you, Jack, and I will continue to do so for the rest of my life. You are under no force to love me back. My words may seem unreal to you, but my feelings for you are absolutely pure and true." Rose says.

All the remaining members of the trekking party clap their hands and cheer. Jack is thoroughly speechless.

"I really appreciate what you feel for me, Rose. Thank you so much! You will always be special to me." Jack says and hugs Rose. The trek comes to an end and all the tourists, including Jack and Rose, return to the hotel. Jack is unable to come to terms with Rose's confession. He feels bad for her. Kathryn's face flashes before his eyes.

"Please forgive me, Rose! My heart beats only for Kathryn." Jack thinks to himself.

5
BACK HOME
RELATIONSHIP WORDS

Jack und Rose sind im Zimmer und packen ihre Koffer. Es ist Sonntagnachmittag. Rose ist verärgert; sie will nicht zurück nach Hause. Ihre **Freunde** und **Kollegen** rufen sie an, aber sie geht nicht ans Telefon.

„Diese Reise hat sehr viel Spaß gemacht. Vielen Dank, Jack", sagt sie.

„Ach, Fräulein Zierlich! Danke mir nicht. Es hat wegen dir Spaß gemacht", bemerkt Jack. „Ich hoffe, dass diese letzte Reise ohne Hürden verläuft", fügt er hinzu.

„Ich hoffe nicht", sagt Rose.

"Was?!"

„Weil ich dadurch mehr Zeit mit dir verbringen kann", sagt sie.

Jack umarmt sie und sagt: „Wir bleiben in Verbindung. Du kannst mich jederzeit anrufen, Rose."

Sie tauschen Nummern aus, woraufhin Rose sagt: „Ich weiß, dass du jetzt nichts für mich empfindest, aber ich bete, dass der Tag sehr bald kommt, an dem du sagen wirst, dass du mich auch liebst."

Jack lächelt.

„Nehmen wir dasselbe Taxi zurück?", fragt Rose.

„Ich kann nicht sagen, ob es dasselbe Taxi sein wird, aber mit Sicherheit derselbe Fahrer."

„Du sagtest, du müsstest zu einer Geburtstagsfeier nach Großbritannien. Um wie viel Uhr geht dein Flug von Florenz?"

„Ich habe noch keinen gebucht. Ich werde den frühestmöglichen Flug nehmen", sagt Jack.

„Ich plane auch, einige Zeit mit meiner **Familie** in der Schweiz zu verbringen", sagt Rose.

„Meine **Mutter** ist sehr böse auf mich, weil ich in letzter Zeit beruflich viel unterwegs war. Ich werde jetzt einige Zeit mit ihr und meinem **Vater** verbringen."

"Hast du **Geschwister**?", fragt Rose.

"Ja. Ich habe eine ältere **Schwester** und eine jüngere Schwester. Meine ältere Schwester ist verheiratet. Sie lebt mit ihrem **Ehemann** in Australien. Die Jüngere malt mit ihrem **Freund** ihre Wohnung rot an", sagt Jack lächelnd.

„Ihr seid eine große Familie. Ich habe nur einen älteren **Bruder** und er ist auch verheiratet. Er lebt mit seiner **Ehefrau** und seinen **Kindern** zusammen mit meinen **Eltern**, meiner **Großmutter** und meinem **Großvater** in der Schweiz.», sagt Rose. „Wann hast du vor, deiner **Freundin** einen Antrag zu machen?", fügt sie hinzu.

"Einen Antrag machen? Ich habe ihr noch nicht einmal gesagt, dass ich sie liebe. Das werde ich an ihrem Geburtstag tun", sagt Jack.

Das Taxi kommt und die beiden fahren nach Florenz. Während sie unterwegs plaudern, sich necken und lachen, erreichen sie Florenz in wenigen Stunden.

„Wir sind endlich in Florenz! Was war das für eine Reise vom Bahnhof in Florenz bis heute!", sagt Jack.

"Ja, wirklich! Von **Fremden** zu Freunden und mehr!

Das war mit Abstand die beste Reise meines Lebens!", sagt Rose.

„Es war wirklich unglaublich! Spaß, Lachen, Abenteuer und viele Pannen!"

„Es war schön, dich kennenzulernen, Jack. Ich werde diese Zeit, die wir zusammen verbracht haben, für immer in Ehren halten. Wie ich dir bereits gesagt habe, werde ich dich für den Rest meines Lebens lieben. Wenn du dich jemals entscheidest, mit Kathryn Schluss zu machen, ruf mich einfach an", sagt Rose.

„Du bist ein wunderbares Mädchen, Rose, nur ein bisschen zierlich! Du wirst immer einen besonderen Platz in meinem Herzen haben. Warten wir ab, was die Zukunft für uns bereithält", sagt Jack und geht zum Flughafen, um seinen Flug nach Großbritannien anzutreten.

Er kommt nach Hause und bereitet sich aufgeregt auf Kathryns Geburtstagsparty an diesem Abend vor. Er bereitet die Geschenke vor und kauft eine besondere Geburtstagskarte für sie. Mit einem großen, wunderschönen Blumenstrauß in der Hand erreicht er Kathryns Geburtstagsfeier. Er entdeckt dort denselben Mann, den er vor ein paar Tagen auf Kathryns Profilbild gesehen hatte. Er beschließt, Kathryn zu fragen, wer er ist.

„Hey Kathryn! Alles Gute zum Geburtstag! Wer ist dieser Mann dort drüben? Ich bin noch nicht mit ihm bekannt gemacht worden. Ich habe ihn vor ein paar Tagen auch auf deinem Profilbild gesehen", sagt Jack.

„Oh, es tut mir so leid, Jack. Lass mich ihn dir vorstellen! Das ist mir komplett durch die Lappen gegangen!", sagt Kathryn und ruft den Mann zu sich.

„Ich wollte euch beide einander vorstellen", sagt sie zu dem Mann. „Das ist Jack, ein sehr enger Freund von mir. Und Jack, das ist Mark, mein **Verlobter**."

Jack ist unglaublich schockiert.

Kathryn lacht und sagt: „Ich wollte alle auf meiner Geburtstagsparty mit dieser Neuigkeit überraschen. Wie gefällt er dir? Ist er nicht wunderbar?"

Jack findet keine Worte. Sein Herz ist in tausend Stücke zersprungen. Er sagt niemandem etwas und verlässt einfach die Party.

Fünf Jahre später ist Jack ein sehr erfolgreicher Schriftsteller. Rose hat auch in der Kunstbranche große Erfolge erzielt. Die Vorhersage trifft ein. Jack und Rose leben glücklich zusammen in einer Villa in London.

SUMMARY

Der Wochenendausflug von Jack und Rose geht zu Ende. Sie sprechen über ihre Familien und lassen die gemeinsamen Stunden der letzten Tage Revue passieren. Rose wiederholt ihre Gefühle für ihn. Sie erreichen Florence und Jack reist nach Großbritannien ab, um an Kathryns Geburtstagsfeier teilzunehmen. Er bereitet sich darauf vor, seine romantische Seite zu zeigen und ihr auf der Party seine Liebe zu gestehen. Als er die Party erreicht, erfährt er, dass Kathryn bereits mit jemand anderem verlobt ist. Jack ist untröstlich und verlässt sofort die Party. Gemäß der Vorhersage des Wahrsagers heiraten Jack und Rose und leben seitdem glücklich zusammen.

WORDS TO REMEMBER

1. **Freunde** - Friends
2. **Kollegen** - Colleagues
3. **Familie** - Family
4. **Mutter** - Mother
5. **Vater** - Father
6. **Geschwister** - Siblings
7. **Schwester** - Sister
8. **Ehemann** - Husband
9. **Freund** - Boyfriend
10. **Bruder** - Brother
11. **Ehefrau** - Wife
12. **Kinder** - Children
13. **Eltern** - Parents
14. **Feste Freundin** - Girlfriend
15. **Fremde** - Strangers
16. **Verlobter** - Fiancé
17. **Großmutter** - Grandmother
18. **Großvater** - Grandfather

QUESTIONS

1. Wie reisen Jack und Rose nach Florenz?

- a. Mit dem Taxi
- b. Zu Fuß
- c. Mit der Straßenbahn
- d. Mit dem Zug

2. Wie viele Geschwister hat Rose?

- a. Zwei Schwestern
- b. Einen Bruder
- c. Zwei Brüder und eine Schwester
- d. Vier Schwestern und fünf Brüder

3. Was macht Jack, nachdem er Florenz erreicht?

- a. Er besucht einen Kunden
- b. Er hat ein Date mit Rose
- c. Er tritt den Flug nach Großbritannien an
- d. Er geht zur Arbeit

4. Was kauft Jack zusätzlich zu den Geschenken für Kathryn zum Geburtstag?

- a. Einen Ananaskuchen
- b. Eine Gedichtsammlung
- c. Ein Auto
- d. Eine Geburtstagskarte

5. Welche überraschenden Neuigkeiten erhält Jack, als er die Party erreicht?

- a. Die Party wurde abgesagt

- b. Rose ist schwanger
- c. Kathryn ist bereits mit jemand anderem verlobt
- d. Kathryn ist verheiratet

ANSWERS

1. **a.** Mit dem Taxi
2. **b.** Einen Bruder
3. **c.** Er besteigt den Flug nach Großbritannien
4. **d.** Eine Geburtstagskarte
5. **c.** Kathryn ist bereits mit jemand anderem verlobt

ENGLISH TRANSLATION

Jack and Rose are in the room packing their bags. It is Sunday afternoon. Rose is upset; she doesn't want to go back home. Her friends and colleagues call her, but she doesn't answer the phone.

"This trip was a lot of fun. Thank you so much, Jack," she says.

"Oh, Miss Petite! Don't thank me. You made it fun." Jack remarks. "I hope this final journey takes place without any hurdles," he adds.

"I wish not," Rose says.

"What?!"

"Because that will give me more time to spend with you," she says.

Jack hugs her and says, "We will be in touch. You can

call me anytime you like, Rose."

They exchange numbers after which Rose says, "I know you don't feel anything for me now, but I pray that day comes very soon when you will say that you love me too."

Jack smiles.

"Are we taking the same cab back?" asks Rose.

"The same cab or not I cannot say, but the same driver for sure."

"You said you have to go to the UK for a birthday party, what time is your flight from Florence?"

"I haven't booked one yet. I will take the earliest flight possible." Jack says.

"I am also planning to go and spend some time with my family in Switzerland," Rose says.

"My mother is very cross with me because I have been traveling a lot for work lately. I will spend some time with her and my father now."

"Do you have any siblings?" Rose asks.

"Yes. I have one elder sister and one younger sister. My elder sister is married. She lives with her husband in Australia. The younger one is busy painting the town red with her boyfriend." Jack says, smiling.

"Yours is a large family. I only have one elder brother and he is married too. He lives with his wife and children in Switzerland along with my parents, my grandmother, and my grandfather." says Rose. "When are you planning to propose to your girlfriend?" she adds.

"Propose! I haven't even told her yet that I love her. I am going to do that on her birthday." Jack says.

The cab arrives and the two of them leave for Florence. While chatting, teasing each other, and laughing along the way, they reach Florence in a few hours.

"We are finally in Florence! What a journey this was,

from the Florence railway station to now!" Jack says.

"Absolutely! From strangers to friends and more! This was by far the best trip of my life!" Rose says.

"It was amazing indeed! Fun, laughter, adventure, and a lot of mishaps!"

"It was lovely getting to know you, Jack. I will forever cherish this time we spent together. As I told you earlier, I will continue to love you for the rest of my life. If you ever decide to break up with Kathryn, just give me a call," says Rose.

"You are a wonderful girl Rose, just a bit petite! You will always hold a special place in my heart. Let's wait and see what the future has in store for us," Jack says and goes to the airport to board his flight to the United Kingdom.

He gets home and excitedly starts getting ready for Kathryn's birthday party that evening. He gets the gifts ready and buys a special birthday card for her. Holding a large, gorgeous bouquet of flowers in his hand, he arrives at Kathryn's birthday party. He spots the same man there that he had seen in Kathryn's display picture a few days ago. He decides to ask Kathryn about him.

"Hey, Kathryn! Happy birthday! Who is that man over there? I've not been introduced to him yet. I also saw him on your display picture a few days ago." Jack asks.

"Oh, I am so sorry Jack. Let me introduce you to him! It completely slipped out of my mind!" Kathryn says and calls the man over.

"I wanted to introduce you both to one another," she says to the man. "He is Jack, a very close friend of mine. And Jack, he is Mark, my fiancé."

Jack is shocked beyond imagination.

Kathryn laughs and says, "I wanted to surprise everyone with this news at my birthday party. How do you like my choice? Isn't it amazing?"

Jack has no words. His heart is shattered into pieces. He says nothing to anyone and just leaves the party.

Five years later, Jack is a very successful writer. Rose has also found great success in the field of art. The prediction comes true. Jack and Rose live together happily in a mansion in London.

CONCLUSION

Congratulations! You have done it!

Reading and understanding a whole story comprising seventeen chapters and several phrases and dialogues in a new language is not easy. Thanks to your efforts, you now know what to say when you meet someone, how to discuss the weather and food, how to ask for directions, how to speak to the salesperson at a shopping mall, how to express your emotions, what to say when you fall in love with someone, and so much more. Through Jack and Rose's story, you have experienced many real-life situations in this new language. You might not have understood each and every word in the book, but what you have accomplished is commendable! You have managed to learn a new language on your own without the help of any teacher and outside of a classroom setting.

Now what?

Now, it's time to practice!

Pick out all those aspects of the book that you didn't understand completely and attempt to master them. Try interacting with a native speaker. Expose yourself to videos, movies, and articles in this new language and try to pick up as much as you can. Every effort you make will take you closer and closer to the ultimate goal of perfection and fluency. No one can learn a language in the space of a few weeks. Even native speakers who are fluent have mastered the language over many years. So, don't feel discouraged. It's normal to find this experience challenging at times, it's normal to forget a few words here and there, and it's normal to make mistakes. Every time you practice, you grow. This gradual growth will eventually take you up there to the pinnacle of success in your language learning journey. Don't give up and don't settle for the ordinary because the best things in life lie on the other side of hard work and patience.

What's next?

There are four books in this series - all packed with short stories and dialogs - that focus on everyday German, ensuring that you learn the basics of the language.

Search for **Language Mastery** to find the rest of the books in the series, as well as dozens of other resources. To continue your language learning journey, simply add the book to your library. We have a book collection, which you can find on your favorite online bookstore or library, that outlines practical steps that you can take to keep learning any language. If you are ever lost or in need of new ideas or direction, we suggest you consult our book collection or just send us an email, we will be there to help you.

Your biggest fan,
Language Mastery!

ALSO BY LANGUAGE MASTERY

SPANISH TITLES

SPANISH 1. **Spanish Short Stories for Beginners:** *Over 100 Conversational Dialogues & Daily Used Phrases to Learn Spanish. Have Fun & Grow Your Vocabulary with Spanish Language Learning Lessons!*

SPANISH 2. **Conversational Spanish Dialogues:** *Over 100 Conversations and Short Stories to Learn the Spanish Language. Grow Your Vocabulary Whilst Having Fun with Daily Used Phrases and Language Learning Lessons!*

SPANISH 3. **Learn Spanish with Short Stories:** *Over 100 Dialogues & Daily Used Phrases to Learn Spanish in no Time. Language Learning Lessons for Beginners to Improve Your Vocabulary & Speak Spanish Like a Native!*

SPANISH BUNDLE. **Learn Spanish for Beginners:** *Over 300 Conversational Dialogues and Daily Used Phrases to Learn Spanish in no Time. Grow Your Vocabulary with Spanish Short Stories & Language Learning Lessons!*

FRENCH TITLES

FRENCH 1. **French Short Stories for Beginners:** *Over 100 Conversational Dialogues & Daily Used Phrases to Learn French. Have Fun & Grow Your Vocabulary with French Language Learning Lessons!*

FRENCH 2. **Conversational French Dialogues:** *Over 100 Conversations and Short Stories to Learn the French Language. Grow Your Vocabulary Whilst Having Fun with Daily Used Phrases and Language Learning Lessons!*

FRENCH 3. **Learn French with Short Stories:** *Over 100 Dialogues & Daily Used Phrases to Learn French in no Time. Language Learning Lessons for Beginners to Improve Your Vocabulary & Speak French Like a Native!*

FRENCH BUNDLE. **Learn French for Beginners:** *Over 300 Conversational Dialogues and Daily Used Phrases to Learn French in no Time. Grow Your Vocabulary with French Short Stories & Language Learning Lessons!*

ITALIAN TITLES

ITALIAN 1. **Italian Short Stories for Beginners:** *Over 100 Conversational Dialogues & Daily Used Phrases to Learn Italian. Have Fun & Grow Your Vocabulary with Italian Language Learning Lessons!*

ITALIAN 2. **Conversational Italian Dialogues:** *Over 100 Conversations and Short Stories to Learn the Italian Language. Grow Your Vocabulary Whilst Having Fun with Daily Used Phrases and Language Learning Lessons!*

ITALIAN 3. **Learn Italian with Short Stories:** *Over 100 Dialogues & Daily Used Phrases to Learn Italian in no Time. Language Learning Lessons for Beginners to Improve Your Vocabulary & Speak Italian Like a Native!*

ITALIAN BUNDLE. **Learn Italian for Beginners:** *Over 300 Conversational Dialogues and Daily Used Phrases to Learn Italian in no Time. Grow Your Vocabulary with Italian Short Stories & Language Learning Lessons!*

GERMAN TITLES

GERMAN 1. **German Short Stories for Beginners:** *Over 100 Conversational Dialogues & Daily Used Phrases to Learn German. Have Fun & Grow Your Vocabulary with German Language Learning Lessons!*

GERMAN 2. **Conversational German Dialogues:** *Over 100 Conversations and Short Stories to Learn the German Language. Grow Your Vocabulary Whilst Having Fun with Daily Used Phrases and Language Learning Lessons!*

GERMAN 3. **Learn German with Short Stories:** *Over 100 Dialogues & Daily Used Phrases to Learn German in no Time. Language Learning Lessons for Beginners to Improve Your Vocabulary & Speak German Like a Native!*

GERMAN BUNDLE. **Learn German for Beginners:** *Over 300 Conversational Dialogues and Daily Used Phrases to Learn German in no Time. Grow Your Vocabulary with German Short Stories & Language Learning Lessons!*

www.ingramcontent.com/pod-product-compliance
Lightning Source LLC
Chambersburg PA
CBHW071914070526
44583CB00016B/1988